The Beautiful Anxiety

The Beautiful Anxiety

Jill Jones

PUNCHER & WATTMANN

First published in 2014
Published by Puncher and Wattmann
PO Box 441
Glebe NSW 2037
http://www.puncherandwattmann.com
puncherandwattmann@bigpond.com

National Library of Australia
Cataloguing-in-Publication entry:

Jones, Jill
The Beautiful Anxiety

ISBN   9781922186430

I. Title.

A821.3
Cover design by Matthew Holt

Printed by McPhersons Printing Group

This project has been assisted by the Australian Government through the Australia Council, its arts funding and advisory body.

Australian Government

Australia Council
for the Arts

For my mother, Norah 1918-2007

dark hides nothing
travelled all these years

winged leaf, stone
life to ground

breath the material
returned light

Contents

Part One: O tasted and gone

Part Two: Wandering breath

Part Three: Which is being too

Part One

O tasted and gone

My Ruined Lyrics

"You forget whole years, and not necessarily the least important ones."
— Javier Marías, *The Dark Back of Time*

1. Hold On

The song isn't as loud
as you think it should be

It accompanies the road
nonetheless

You hear it in the rain

Hang on, even a cicada has got
its dream rhythm

That walks with you
through the door

After you've crossed the river
look back, it's passed you

The notes trail

Its attributes are lies and truth
the clash of pasts

2. I'm Coming

I can't give you any more
although the weir overflows

And here in my pockets
another flow

Of cellophane, an old musket
a slide rule, seed catalogues, powers

The river rises
in the hundred year flood

There's something planetary
in the moan of levees

I lay my hands on
evidence changing gears

My logbook is full of
sneaky miles

The lie is of the tongue

And I would kiss you with it
when I come

3. Fields of Wheat

The hour is a vast frontier
moving into day.
In it I spent a year
and then a decade
moving you all around.

It was all down to
bad timing at a desk
the design of borders
a lack of motivation and petrol
and now the Russians have come
with gold lamé g-strings
and a kind of unattractive
comedy
that beats queuing.

I know these are dreams of salvage
and dawn the rescue hour
climbing stairs into duties.
But the orders are confused
and nothing seems to grow.

I ask the Russians for true grain
and a giant sleigh
but it's become too warm
and foghorns tumble.

It is each according to need
and the sun strikes up the band.

4. Bird on the Run

Somewhere the war
is outside my window
showing on a graph
heart-shaped
and inevitable.
But I do not roar in pain
yet.

I am waiting for the birds
then I'll know.
They are not a chorus.
They do not know
how to come home.
They no longer bear
the message.

Which is why

    I jump the sill
    I jump the rocket launcher.

    I jump the map

and it bears me.

      Hear my wings!

5. Flesh and Spark

And when I came
to you
it was raining

We had to be covered
in something other
than ink-black night

The guitars had all drifted
in their boats
animals were nervous

If we don't get access
there's still
recall, its open moment

Along the curled map
of seeds
and their prices

Among the shot
the falling lead
and winged cartography

There, let us have
our doubts
we grave them secret skins

Though covered
they tell flesh
and spark

6. Unusual

The air fills with
petrichor
after rain on sandstone.

It's unusual, and we must
speak it
this drought, this daring.

It will be fire.
It will be cord and rope.
We'll sing it long.

The war wasn't a lie.
The bombs dropped ... so.
And near where you told me.

Trace it on the sheet
and this once
dream it on the beach.

Then outside awakened
again we walk in the depth

of field.

Wave

The traffic begins its wave,
the sky is threaded with exhaust,
the blind man has a ticket, your bag
is heavy today, the traffic is beautiful
going somewhere, the sky does not move
though it seems to, the hours begin
to waver, you begin to think of effort
and time, the endless hatcheries
of capital, the blind man knows the way,
the traffic is heavy with somewhere,
the sky is beautiful though
it doesn't seem so, the hours thread
with tickets or numbers.
The numbers are beautiful,
rolling along like waves.
And in afternoon the blind man
waits with you, the sky is endless
but it is not, the traffic is threaded
with numbers, each ticket is beautiful
within its own exhaust.

What's Coming Next

We are coughing because the train is late.
Someone still wears a volunteer's uniform.

The tabloids have all had coupons torn from them.
Maybe it's easier to focus on cloudy days.

No use worrying, the results are in.
Do dreams stand up in the slashing gravel?

An expensive perfume arises out of damp air.
There's the smell of a fire sale.

An age is coming of slow intrinsic diseases.
No matter how long he stares at the map, the carriage falters.

What worked then and what's working now?
Equivalence is in the magic.

In the glass is another world.
You can bare silence and find it neither golden nor clear.

If today is streaky, tomorrow will be unreasonable.
There's a long street where leaves are tipped red.

The peace gets more anxious.
'For sale' signs are out, stapled on plywood.

All bets are off.
You have to go through it.

Pages of legal clauses have upset the momentum of speech.
Functionaries run towards the rain with buckets.

The Weight

I go out without saying
with all my haul to come back
in between, criticism and measure
the timing of the lights
how cold the upright steel how cold
the headlines pile up just like saying
there's less difference now
though bread seems various at a distance
packets are wondrous as we attend
within the fleeting
you hear my shoes do their own talking
on terrazzo and perhaps there's fair price to pay
perhaps it makes no difference
the blue bag fills with supermarket krill
it's automatic in the queue of special words
you lift the coin onto your tongue
this is the expectation
I only get so far praying extra
the walk back seems longer than my feet
can I spit money into the dying pool

Misinterpretations /or The Dark Grey Outline

I move through a slanting,
footpaths erupting roots through bricks
near the mad old bus stop.
I used to know what I was thinking,
now it's a field, inside,
is it green, or grey water, horsing,
gridding,
heavens bent
through the fleck.
Sometimes I wonder if I'm drinking the wrong water,
the other day I read
I had a sort of degree, but I ain't, no way *Hose-Bloody-Zay*.
Please, I-am-not-a-doctor,
I'm too unfashionable for that.

Even in Sydney when days get cuter
than cop cars, as the city train smells of its electricity
and cut-up vinyl,
makes you want to chisel rocks with letters,
makes you think, placing As while breathing
Hawkesbury sandstone,
oh gritty gritty something,
don't let go.

But from Greenhill Road I can see a Dark Grey Outline,
gums on the Toorak Gardens horizon
after rain pins on Portrush,
windy,
juggle juggle,
that's the bus tyres.

Tickets are eaten,
baskets savaged, cars dinking in line.
It seems average but sounds pushy
out the window,
my eyes scram down choosing the wet leaf
blown onto a white roundabout.
Something I learned when I was young,
shape is serious matter.
I am not what I'm supposed to be.
Light is spring silver
and escapes my language,
in the next lane
'fragile goods'.

Outside a North Terrace carpark
is the Ha-Ha Arrow,
pointing white blue charge grips,
tinker tinker bus blows money,
odd jangles of student housing,
arrivals not quite fusion (Go Backwards).

The second lift won't stop
at the fifth floor,
'it's worth reporting'. What, corridors?
In here, it's ice white as carpet,
closing time.
If you don't approve,
or burn, 'therefore'.
Perhaps I am Missing Pages Out Of My Life.
I've always been flaky, lost and shaky,
but never 'ponderous' over my territory,
that takes planning.
It's always been weather not

geosophy (that's so fashionable! yeah?).
I'm delicate, sandy,
unknown, please, or 'to not know',
falling without finding.

But what am I thinking, of giving up the desk,
going off-road, gravelling, dirt thrash?
Why not, given the green's mixed up,
weather rattled, promises running off
leaves as prediction pouring through vents.

The creeks are high,
snake tongues, feathers,
water calls, absolutely
and briefly,
tomorrow forks
but for now
full cold moon
and wrestling night.

I have dreamed green tiles,
walls, gaps, dirty grassy
penalty signs,
curves, yes, finally,
pink ankle
and all this air, all this.

If I'm not what I'm supposed to be
then why all this certainty,
how do I escape its cackling old *Sprache*?

Night in Frome Road
is there at its hour,

cold erupting through asphalt,
sight and feeling mashed with
my flaking alphabets.

The Future

How massive seems the sky inflated with pages,
fever folded into piffle journalism, it is more
than to be coped with. *Come love me then
if thou art famished.* If the fire has gone from art.

And music, well, its dire straits are everywhere,
the nurture of tattoos across kid bellies,
each fresh in the white discharge of phoneland,
distext of modern teeth and tongues.

If I'm receiving you that I may be filled.

And later, to be kissed by the sea
amongst salt and dogs, a bulging sun.

Our hunger swoops upon our dreams.
The revolution is in the messagebank.
Taste the devil's details! And let's see.

Collect

Dust the everpresent
floats, sticks
makes up
making
unmaking

Dust, clever dust, visiting
surfaces

I see through it
or brush past it

Reality, ephemera, the screen
is heavier than a fine
taste
particulate to tongue
flaw and fleck

If you are heavier than dust
it does not mean more

Trees, bricks, glass – careful – see what
you see through fine
scum skirting
corner, the eye grit

Veil quiet
handed through
light flirting

Bed, table, window, path,
exit into the day dust
gust up

Control is
to corner dust
cover and uncover and cover
dust is too hard, too fine

I'm fine when I see
the pattern
the not-pattern the fall of
an afternoon
moving into the
smoother
timing of this
rain

Myriad
miasma making
chimera making
lining sanctuaries
no ghosts but the ghost
of all

Dread like sheet to discover
what they hid from you
not surprise
and candle burns it through
passages, tracing

Minute, evanescent
moveable

the brush-off
kicking crust
to bite, to kick, to eat
dust

Subatomic
where will this end

Genres of dust
dust bowl
red dust at the centre
across the whiteness
salt, sand, chalk
damm, dreck, tierra

What can you see
the small, see
fall and see

It is *la,* a, tha, *ein, continuo*

Here is trembling
watch the escape
discern, discern
there's something
terrible
in all this

Generations of dust
from 1815 to 1816
dust covers the world
Mount Tambora giving dark
to mellow fruitfulness

1954, dust glows over Bikini

All the ash Wednesdays
firing dust
war dust, extinction dust
disgusting dust

Salt-filled dusty wind
destroy, to make

Walk into the day, that tomb
of dead living
on fabric
textile of
places, shoulders
dry, the corners
discard, disturb

Someone magnifies
particles, peat
dust rocks on
rocks
these degrees, how you
place a gaze
onto the degree
of matter
matters

Vastness
loess
in a grain
clay, cells
realms

hermetic

Filling spaces, endless space
planets of dust
galaxy up until dust
miniatures, universe
flying out of great dust

My hand is always to touch
worlds of

There is no lonely dust

Turns On Water

My day leaks or leaps
nonetheless it turns
on water or its lack at the fence
where the ground is feedy
and in or after all matter
is weedy growth
what happens in cracks
language both outside and inside
but who attempts these words
who stamps out the weeds
these things replicate and carve
a way into bones, a path
a movement down the slope
or along the retaining wall
as though each has within
a model that's cloven
into it water flows and is
rapt into ground making of it
rivulets water maps shadowy deltas
reasons as if there were too many
counting the day and all
its green coverage moulds
and litter veils without glamour
clear water building strength
layers in frothing
never remains

Grids

There's a stranger approaching
on the gravel and
air between decisions
themselves and the imagined.

My shoulders are pushing nothing
at mis-communication
the gift of crouching
a state or a yellow headache.
They're not an indigo dream.

Into morning's crush
of new speedways I make
in the pixellated gait
lies but they're hard.
Intentions and motives are not
that grids cross over.

And bones, and salmon-
coloured aura of rivers and seas
that's between my breath.
For the ephemeral world
there's barely words.

I would shake his hand
as if truly here.

Some (   ) Time

fragile tears or strong enough falling
all
that's left
the uncertain lengths

there are possibles, rain on earth
lacunae
and lostness
but are everywhere

and to hear crackles of diodes
think
of a
few recovered scraps

ardent/ ears/ eyes, the taste, skin
some future time
will think
?

ache in time along with leaves

- with a fragment from a fragment of Sappho

Impermanent Tenses

1
I watch myself
lost inside myself
glass
the skin
mistakes of language

Talking within each
other in pursuit
our
own best
and holy season

I give up
in the stroke
the
body fails
even its excuses

Many ways to
talk through pulp
self's
changing ratio
letterbox pan widescreen

Hear little stings
from phones redundant
testing
situation with
the real/ word

Life takes place
on planets sleek
smoky
we travel
our uncertain seats

Cheeky corners render
moments of
disappearance

2
Our staggering stuff in nested containers
excess looking back while going forward

Silent or sung
too little being
graffiti
creaking rail
the hissing pneumos

Volcanoes sound lava from old women
cradled in their mouths and lyrics
quilts culture above the minimalist abyss

Voices dolcissimo marzipan
a little more
dreamt
of original
bliss letting the

Pleasure go 'way
out' signs past

The Beautiful Anxiety

The paths are full of iron and stars.
Who does not welcome all this
black, burning with misplaced rain?
If it's reported that islands have gone
missing, remember how seas love us
and trail in our blood.
If there's too much of a ghost now
upon the clouds, a wing, a roar
none of that will open
the dead to this world again.

There's nothing purely accidental
in your edgy condition.
Damage seems almost a necessity.
If there's beauty in patina, it's here
not just waiting for the cracks
in the permanent. It's subcutaneous
like a language that entered you
without stamps of approval.

You step out with your necessity
because nothing will grow within
houses for too long.
Your sandals and heels, your capped toes
they are some kind of assurance
along with the belated rain, whose water
slaps the ridges of your song.

Each tree that wasn't there before
each element or fibre, the occasional feather

or slip of whitened excrement
the glassy tips of plastic that flutter
as you pass, they are places.
Hands have admitted them
and their appearances
have depended on each isobar and swell
of time zones.

You must be going elsewhere
see how it skews the horizon and adds
something green to the temperature.
There are instruments for this
kind of knowing, along with bright machines
moving tonnage along temporary roads.

But if you can still turn your hand around
the rain and touch skin's rearranging
of its walking —

figures
atoms
curves
droplets

and distinguish the cold of it, dropt on
sun shadows within the petrochemical hum
its erotic scent, a ghost of ash
passing stars, and a kind of subliminal speech
among legends of flowers and birds, roses
of the place where the phoenix plays
that useless search within the art of speech
to fly amongst lost things again
the long road from the north

hard sails built out of trawl.

There's never time to know
yourself. That's the beautiful anxiety
of moving, as each gutter, each wing
each clip, or semiconductor
the air dripping through your skeleton
your fur that scares easily, as it all
seems to be crashing.

The air moves history into history.
You look where leaves hold the light
skin holds the light
edges hold the light.

Nothing holds on
the light.

Big Fun

I died for fun
under the mask of the fair.
My hand still holds its line.
That's the joke!
My dress in fullness cries down.

Who will quarrel over it?
The square eyes, machine jaws.

Fireworks line the eastern sky.
Even more ferocious
the bitter south sea
the blasted sandhills, the end
of a million year fête.

Who will quarrel over it?
Whose machines, whose eyes?

My Green Name

Instructions are the death
in this age of phoney wars.
The measurement of roads is moveable.
There's a humming in the mangroves
while the building is shaking
and rain crashes like a bomb.

If I knew my name, like that song
— remember how it went —
a red wisp of thought
before you step onto the path.
Once the cordons are down
it slips past and flowers wild
in the cracks of an obelisk.

Though sky is soothed by ground
the leaves are not mistaken.
Dry grass and yearning hears me
or I am barefoot among stacks
turning green in the wind.

Six Temperamental Sonnets

1.
Signs & Portents

Finally you're faced with a sign
that says "free beer", and some one is yelling
"put th'boot in" — it's not like your mother
said as she soothed the knots in your head.

One day some books will speak about us
if there are books and another "us"
which didn't go soft like a pashmina shawl
at the end of the path, as winter chugs over
the bandstand and we're kissing on the grass
ignoring time and its mate, the lunar wash.

Someone with cobalt hair attacks the rain
with a kind of "bottoms up" fervour.
But we stay inattentive, our body heat catching
us, and this is still important.

2.
Luck

Is it enough to possess such things,
the equivalent or the local? Is a leaf
enough to translate its world, or will
a pressure of wings enslave the beholder,
in fervent, continuous mouthing of enigmas,
less intelligent than elephants in summer mud?

Longitudes, Mediterraneans, species! Now
is the hour for a poetry of remarkable absences.

Therefore, take an inch of an antidote
for the extended and zealous flashes
of the whiteman in heat, while we hunger
for the original sap within the rock.

Whoever has the lucky ticket should leap
into what's left of each wave and tree.

3.
Whale Songs

Insurance lends a hand to the dream
but the dice is pretty much the way it is,
pretty much like the famous dog and its day,
just as driving an old Taurus takes guts,
you'll need at least fourteen portions
of crystal and bat sheen, gingery flooze.

All those blustering gentlemen, shining
balls on their whites, still can't play
it straight in an uncomfortable clime
at the end of ages, as the whales approach,
now on foot and inconsolable, unable
to digest the folderol of the high seas.

The ice slides into disrepair and the acid city
finally measures the alarm.

4.

Insufficiency

Any pain the book can repair
has lost out to chronology's fashion.
There's annunciation under rain
the talk of an end to work
though much of the ground is disowned.

This isn't a preliminary, no sir
we have the requisites and the excess.
Though our good will's gone hunting
heaven's special stays on message.
The old becomes extraneous
the sufficient is simple and pleasant
even in our pretty uniforms.

Youth is approximate if not
the time that loves you.

5.

Summer Holiday Charms

Dreams fill with letters, chockers with transition.
Do you get the sea change, lazy lagoons,
dogs running at the big tide, like old bulls?
The dead man's chest is shining, preened
with coconut oil and foamy precipitates.

Once we were lording it over time
our feet sensitive to lava and doubt's trip
over the shaky levels, countdowns,
the way the pub band yells, hey kerang!

There's nothing ardent amongst skinny shrubs
the sweet and sour balancing on paper plates.
There's always a critic in a room flushed with smoke
and narky bandits, checking you, mate,
unhanded. Like, fuck significance!

6.

Finally, Whispers!

With just a little science we can disturb much
in the time-space continuum
if you stay beautiful, and I'm steady, game
in the gravel — rendered from loneliness
my world pushes its conundrums, worming
clarity, dumb intelligence, animal feeling.

Do you remember how it felt after
the motion, or the mediation? Will it be
the goods or their absence, massive temperatures
between thighs, oceans and hot abdomens
sarin gas, river fevers, flash memory, girlie flush.
It's guts, glory, then we're famished, o tasted and gone!

Diversions, combustions, the changa-chang
everywhere! White teeth, sloppy kisses. Such words!

Seven Types of Knowledge

Interior
morning register
exaggerates daily danger.

Therefore
to end
where existence enters.

Knowledge's
internal conclusions
vibrate considered rain.

Given
yesterday's regulations
the embers began.

Collapse
of forms
an outside possibility.

Abundance
equips fabric
this outside broken.

Chronometer
drops ash.
Here's the rise!

As It Comes To You, Finally

I see smoke loops by trees
and hear voices of those
arrested and pursued.
There's an injury
which certainly must break us.
This is as sure as everything.
That flashing isn't gold
or stairs within the sky.
The whole air is burning
with extremity.

We would wish to be safe,
repair the wall or the information
but these times are writing
into the Substance.
So a day will be taken to its lengths
when, in misgiving,
the last forests give form
to these chains, our echoes.

The road we roll on
is greater than our parts.
In order to act, begin
this walk into the Whole, and sing
with a clear woman who gives
return for the felt hard air,
for the shadow.

To connect, let the wind
clear your lies and your whispers.

(All memory knows the word,
the end for which is come.)

Dear injury, can you hear
how the storms are blowing?
Listen hard as it comes to you finally.

If we're all at a cliff and a balance
. . .
to break ourselves of everything.

A White Boat

A moment sings your hard life
against the pier

A voice dreams your thought
your spirit with all its riot

Music moves through night
a city lodges in you

A figure walks alone
disturbing order

Your corpse enters
reminiscent of all aphrodisiacs.

Not every road is a possible road
since you ruined time

Each judgment has its secrecy
the shutdowns of therefore

Each possible way
will destroy and endure, only you

Even in that moment
the white boat is here, for you.

Part Two

Wandering breath

Skin

I went out
to stand in the rain
as if falling
felt any different
outside
among things you
didn't dream about

dandelion
or plastic

appearances
appear whether real
water smells
like it's here
what skin is
for or the tongue or

both

In Hours

Bird dream gone
past rain, past
lies, motives, niches

Home not home
till you flee
reject stupid traffic

Wish for wing
sky, rain or
xerox your zeppelins

In rich air
roll fast hours
upon vagrant wastes

Air

The air bites shrewdly
it is very cold

my other elements
which, but for vacancy

as sweet as balm, as soft as
contagious darkness

For now sits expectation
with colours idly spread

promise-crammed
splitting the air with noise

Remainders

Go get you home
in hard voyages
guarded with scraps
the bits, and greasy relics.

Nay, you were
some slender ort
From whence,
fragment?

Recoveries

Cloud crowd out
watch channel
monitors somewhere souls savvy

corridors shadow opium
intrude ghost idea
tomorrow code escape

now unleashed lagoon
wind fugitives
fluid wings move levels

Dark Clangs Down

material quivers ever
something away
underneath

patterns breeze
place
unravels moving

Chains

chains perforate fear
how they align

data extended to
shackles companies borders

clutch prohibits repair
layers equip experts

where substance ends
arrive, touch chains

it's easy to
be executed, accumulated

inconsolable the tangent
of a sigh

The Futures

To
learn branch
secret wood's sadness

day
finishes me
approximately in fog

fire's
speech method
impossible outside time

how
much is
polished extinguished distant

ask
here future
with each colour

brush
inflects error
the white plenty

'The air will tell us'

Strings, forms, necessity
break continually,
material
shapes
immaterial.

Cave, candlewax, tears
twanging
silky, brilliant brooding
flesh.
Johann! Laura!

Blowfly, rainbow, scrub
whispers legend
mortally, eternal
disturbing
white trivialities.

Henceforth, air
Sprachen
blau, Himmel.

— *Patched from 'Voss'*

New Sight

As there is new silence there is desire

As there is new slope there is difference

As there is new smoke there is debate

As there is new spell there is dioxide

As there is new software there is dust

As there is new sight there is drift

Wide

Not water but distance
widens in the waking
Moons are not decisions
They are gaps of light
timing little boats
I take
each time the tune turns
to face its origin

I Am, I

I am, I am a little, I am
a parcel, I am yet
I dreamed this mortal
I grew up bent

I had a picture, I hear a river
I like a ship in storms, I put
your leaves aside, I remember
the clumsy

I saw the spiders, I struck
the board, I that have been
I, too, I wrote in
the dark

Part Three

Which is being too

About Directions

Because of this I am almost a man
because of this I am almost a leaf
because of this I am almost a wave
or a particle, a portion of stone
something impurely electric, almost
and even, in the rain that washes off
skin and runs like faint blood
in my hair, because in the end
out on this spit, this thinned strait
this slightly landed place, because
I am almost none of these things
and the lights go out slowly
beyond the promenade and houses
sleep and I take your hand and
place it where my throat aches to
say as a woman in a place
though you let the wind push you
about directions as they change do not
emerge from the sea unmoved but
say as a woman let us, and let us
because we are almost there
you can see where the valley cleaves
almost in twain and surge
so much colder than your hand
washes atrophy into ocean

Erosions

Your dreams erode me.
I'm tired of standing anyway.
I've already left my attitude
dream-thrust
above houses of the holy.
I'm with the lightning
the pink power of which
you're always afraid.

Can we call it quits?
Let me move into lands
beyond the frame
and you into your own love.

If I have a place, there it is
an open plain, beyond
walls and chasms
or erratic, androgynous truths
that figured you
the sea we come from.

Don't forget my playful hollows.
Give me back my hands.
No dream stands outside of history.

The Tender Stone

The pen so cold
snow edging the city
wind tests the monuments
their verdigris work of the soul.

There'll always be dancing
at the *bar americain*
though the tongue freezes
without speech.

All along the boulevard
people press their lives
into the sounds
in their heads.

There's something tender in stone
cold frees it
the living stand with flowers
feel the coming sleet.

Water is more than rain
There's no sleep beyond the night
and now is always interruption
sweeping away leaves.

I cover my head
where the cold falls.

Cimetière Montparnasse

Big Flower

I haven't had that dream again
night visitor death and the big flower
I did not even die but rose
through the strata, plains of clouds
beams, quivers, satellites, walkers
to the place the moon might be
somewhere around earth but
just a slip eastward, northward
in the shaky sky beyond the sky
where the birds come from where
they all talked on the ground
before trees looked like trees
when I was young I dreamed of
tunnels, of walking passages
of hydrangeas to blue-green death
but I did not die I flew
I thought this proved something
or would make me content with
the way things were, wearisome
worthwhile or perhaps just wonky.

Death knows me, the moon knows
me, I see that smile on the birds
that know me in the tree
to the northeast, me, their bright
bodies the least of my preparations.

Recipe/ Fluffed And Begging Out of This

It gets confusing when the recipe
calls for three cups and ups the strain.
I inflict myself with abilities I don't have.
In each bowl there's something sifted, fluffed
and begging out of each cupboard.
One wants to be green, but flames turn every particle
into another fume. Brown, brown flour
does not taste so lovely as its bread.

It's not funny, I don't understand how to breed
measurements out of each cupboard and
there's something begging through this.
I want it to be green but flames turn
every particle into another brown
which does not taste so lovely as its cheeky cakes.

It's not funny breeding measurements
out of this. There are flames I don't have
and require questions, or get myself confused
when the recipe calls for three hands, one
of them in the cupboard, lovely as its cheeky spoons.

Someone splices a broom to correct the strain.
I inflict myself with measurements
and ladle myself into another fume.
I've only taken on spoons and get myself
fluffed with abilities. There are names given
I should have taken with two hands, one of them left.

There is something fluffed,
begging out of this cup.
There are bowls I should have taken,
but over my shoulder
I spoon the ups of each cupboard.
I lick myself out of corners.

The Spare Winter

Each week the weather spirals
cold on the rails. The blue falls.
I've pinned hopes on a ticket away
closed my door on the Snowy winds.
The camellia gave up two flowers, alone
I write myself into mystery at the window.
I gather simpler things on the plate
and count the birds I've missed in the strife.

Each day tendencies breach headphones
no-one sits among silence.
In deep city thralls there's a kind of happiness
at each counter something ordinary and bright.
'Praise and blame belong to youth and glory.'
Even a pair of sneakers grows old quick.
Winter rain can almost manage its balm
the black cat softens the iron roof.

Misplaced

Sometimes the poem is
out of order
or in the other air
when it is hotter
placed after before
in the evening.
The moon shines on
the day, the sun
sinks elsewhere
and the page is lit
by the evening star
which was not lost
even after all
those blanket years
city lights, summer snow
and the return
of the albatross
gliding within storms
as the southern ocean
tosses its spray
onto ropes, canvas
the rocks, the mainland
rearranging the page.

Keen

The Past
Hanging out
   the doors of trains

Light is yellow, sky spare
I can't hide

School
   worst thing is
I don't remember

The punt: A woman in matador pants whose leg was bleeding

The maple
   dawn
      passes

The black road
killers/ passengers
   into the hours

Spring
You know how it goes
   planting, reaping weeds

Head aches
sun hangs on the hill

SURPLUS
Words and wine

Birds fly out of walls
pages sound on the floor

SWEAT
Season when it's impossible

HISTORY
Outliving limits

Window
Air stings your lips, what kiss -
    to free you?

Infernal consumption
    deep
doting fire

TRUST
Wooden fences

Murder scene
We fell over the edge
　　into prime time

In the west
An anaemic slot of sky
hesitation of a train

Butch/femme
Green 12 year-olds
hesitating over our limits

Pale skin and freckles: She liked me but she moved to the country

TONE
chokes on keening divas

Club Kooky
drinking
from the mouths of strangers

The hallway is lit
night runs into it

Flight of the material
a cold white bed

Bone matrix
My crappy veins
   hide in soft tissue

Moon bone
dark nuzzle
   nerve light
      on your hand

Dream
Flesh undermines itself
I wait for a softer landing

Voice
As often as she made the gig
you'd look around (don't look)

Summer: Dry comments across ground

The hill
This spiked rain

Listening To 'Quatuor pour la fin du temps' On a Rainy Night In Sydney

Unseasonal rain drowns the
final note, *tempus edax rerum.*
It's an ending, the body of
the god created
gets beyond the screen.

Now, without sleep, without
waking, the irrelevancies
continue swimming to paradise.
Do you know where we are?
That the end is ecstasy?

Techniques and guardians,
locks and keys, 'indefectible light',
in slow repeats of rain or sped-up
storms, leaves bearing water,
climate changing summer.
Perhaps an angel 'qui annonce'
lava and stars, the coming of seas
amongst us.

'That there should be time no longer'?

'And I saw another mighty angel'
not just in the air descending
but clouding the age
'from sun fire
completing a mystery'
out of what was found.

Along the road, there's no
slamming brakes, only
some swearing just
so you know

what 'shall begin to sound'?

This Time

I like the poison
but blood wears itself
out anyway
stuck in the midst
of old skies
ancient gipsy on the run

but this time high
above the planet
spinning around hurts
the heart
its valves who would
be pink in the darkness.

Urn

I don't know
where to put you.
Here is the Nothing.
It's an old country
shaped by dreads and births.

Never end, never end.
The wide plains have eaten us.

Down the river I will go
but not entirely with you.
Slowly along the bank
blood moves to ash
and becomes the
memory's planet.

This is one fight
you win by losing.

The Dress Sonnet

I have taken off my little dress, there's no scope
for me within it, there are things
that fall down the body, like breath and the texture
of the flap. This is a button I can't do.
I don't want to argue on the easy side. 'Don't expect
an audience or a reveal.' O, the little dress
shimmers in the near breeze as I'm falling down
my body and, at last with my ear to the ground

it's too late in the season to please as wind removes
my feathers and shaves my bones with that first whip
of change, and each winter, if it comes along, do I
need its great coat, will I have done with cumbered sleeves?
Sometimes I could do with the humour of a petticoat.
O, let me part the clouds, let me in.

My Beautiful Misfortunes

My internal commandos subvert
my intentions, how worrisome
this discord, and your asterisks.
Do you mean to refuse me
and all my internal merchandise?

Despite this, my lady,
my overseer of nightly encounters,
the milkshake through my dream life,
the jump start of my kismet,
may I weave you errant songs
out of my hidden stocks,
my estopped denials?

Lady, if we don't finish, then
we can begin. I could sing
out loud: "I won with
my misfortune!" a love without
dissembly, now I've thrown
sensible shoes away into old choruses.

At last, without conventional clothes
I lift ineffable discoveries,
all your colours are mutable,
and that destroys me into dancing.

This Is Not Dove Cottage

The house is talking dirty, it's that time of night
when heat goes off the naked ceiling,
& closer & closer, step by step,
wood gets hold of the plaster,

& it's better to be with you in Sydney.
My books, sure, are large with lakes & grandeur,
tramping the vale's good for thinking,
but the heat of your arm is more than thought.

I wish the house would smile,
I wish Wordsworth had
had a sense of humour, or stayed with his
French *maîtresse*, what was her name - *Annette* -

we could talk then, take our time, lakes are
far from here & air fills with
irregular ticks, you are far from here,
the house fills with dirty noisy cold, somewhere

there's a joke in this that never made it back
into revolution, *bon hiver* is
stretching the point,
what is your hand doing over there?

Sensate

Apricots a
kind of
balance

it's seasons
you can't smell
this forever

grapes break
slowly
in your hand

and then sweet
and then swell
as below

leaves
the tongue
a word catches

there's sinew
leakage
skin organs

and you
play
a little

tough
it in the breeze
before

all that outside
which is
being too

The Slide

Sometimes they put you in seas
or rivers without telling you.
The river is dark, let's say
and trees are low over you.
In the branches are owls
making noises like a machine
breathing.

After you come away from this
you have a scar and a jar
where you swim.
It is chemical, archaeological
and violent.

So you wash it all away.
It's too early for things to be
broken or twisted
but even when you run, you fall.

All your life, if you could fly
all your life slides from under you
and you do not have to swallow
water or hear it.

You do not have to but you must
as the clouds fall without telling you.

Trees

If night always comes
what does this say
about anything
that returns,
that slips the line.
Are you ready to discuss
what happens
one night, any night
in its swamps
in its hardness or soft
slow, grainy agreement
with anything better
than here?
There's evidence of rain.
They measure it in
cups like blood
and wind caught
in balloons and lungs.
There's nothing you can
say about night
that hasn't been said,
dreams, horrors
all that banal dark stuff.
Night goes into day.
Nothing goes alone
as it is.
Some nights are made up
not with dreams
but endlessness.
You do and you do

till it's not done.
Hello sunrise, let's
keep going. Recall is
pointless now.
Dawn always has witnesses.
These trees go on
for some while.

In Air

Move slowly and compose in air
Your mind walks with ghosts on the ceiling

Stand as you move into your limbs
Love your fences and stone as you may

There's no reply that won't hurt you

Notes To Poems

My Ruined Lyrics: 'petrichor' is the term coined in 1964 by two Australian scientists, I.J. Bear and R.G. Thomas, to denote the smell of rain on dry ground; see *Nature* 201, 993 (1964).

As it Comes To You, Finally: after 'Inside the Words of Stairway to Heaven' (textile and thread) by Lucille Martin, and a series of photographs by Ted Harvey of the 1972 Led Zeppelin Sydney concert.

Air and *Remainders*: consist entirely of words and phrases from the plays of Shakespeare.

'The air will tell us': after 'Cover design for Voss' by Sidney Nolan. Each word in the poem also appears separately somewhere in the Patrick White novel, *Voss*. The poem's title is spoken by the character, Laura Trevelyan, in the novel.

'I am, I' – composed of phrases from poems by John Donne, 'Holy Sonnets', Henry David Thoreau, 'I Am a Parcel of Vain Strivings Tied', John Clare, 'I am', Robert Herrick, 'The Vine', Charles Simic, 'Prodigy', Charles Wright, 'Homage to Claude Lorraine', Trumbull Stickney, 'Fragment IX', John Gay, 'The Beggar's Opera', Amy Lowell, 'The Weather-Cock Points South', Weldon Kees, 'For H.V.', Robert Lowell, 'Mr Edwards and the Spider', George Herbert, 'The Collar', Ben Jonson, 'A Sonnet to the Noble Lady...', Marianne Moore, 'Poetry', Malcolm Lowry, 'Strange Type'.

Erosions: after 'The Attitude of Lightning Toward a Lady Mountain' by James Gleeson.

The Spare Winter: contains a line translated from Du Fu.

Listening To 'Quatuor pour la fin du temps' On a Rainy Night In Sydney: contains quotes from Olivier Messiaen's notes on his work 'Quatuor pour la fin du temps' including phrases from The Book of Revelation.

Acknowledgments

The following poems, often in different forms, were first published in the print and online journals, chapbooks and anthologies noted below, and my thanks go to their editors:

'My Ruined Lyrics' in *Salt* (UK); 'Wave' in *The Australian*; 'What's Coming Next' in *papertiger*; 'The Weight', 'Six Temperamental Sonnets' in *Otoliths*; 'Misinterpretations /or The Dark Grey Outline' in *Overland*; 'The Future' in *The Warwick Review* (UK); 'Grids', 'Recipe/ Fluffed And Begging Out Of This', 'This Time' in *Rabbit*; 'Some ( ) Time' in *The Hay(na)ku Anthology, Vol II*, eds Jean Vengua & Mark Young, Meritage Press and xPress(ed), 2008 (USA/Finland); 'Impermanent Tenses' in *The First Hay(na)ku Anthology*, eds Mark Young & Jean Vengua, Meritage/X-Pressed, 2005 (USA/Finland); 'The Beautiful Anxiety' in *4W*; 'My Green Name' in *Agenda* (UK); 'Seven Types of Knowledge' in *MiPoesias* (USA); 'As It Comes to You, Finally', 'A White Boat' in *Horizon* (UK); 'Dark Clangs Down', 'Wide' in *Moria* (USA); 'Chains' in *The Famous Reporter*; 'The Futures' in *listenlight* (USA); 'I Am, I', 'Big Fun', in *foam:e*; 'About Directions' in *Vlak* (Czech Repub); 'The Spare Winter', 'My Beautiful Misfortunes' in *Southerly*; 'The Tender Stone' in *Heat*; 'Big Flower' in *The Poet's Quest for God*, eds Oliver Brennan and Todd Swift, Eyewear Press, London, 2014; 'Misplaced' in *322 Review* (USA); 'Keen' in *Muse Apprentice Guild* (USA); 'Listening To 'Quatuor pour la fin du temps' On a Rainy Night in Sydney' in *Ekleksographia* (Japan); 'Urn' in *Meanjin*; 'The Dress Sonnet' in *Over There: Poems from Singapore and Australia*, eds John Kinsella and Alvin Pang, Ethos Books, Singapore, 2007; 'This Is Not Dove Cottage' in *Jacket*; 'The Slide' in *Westerly*; 'In Air' in *The Australian Literary Review*.

'Erosions' was part of a series of ekphrastic poems which appeared in the Rare Objects chapbook, *Fold Unfold*, Vagabond Press, 2005. In turn, this and a number of other poems were first written for performance and booklet publication for the DiVerse poets group who have been involved for a number of years in writing in response to various visual arts exhibitions and events, primarily in Sydney. My thanks to Robert Kennedy and all my fellow DiVerse poets over the years.

'My Ruined Lyrics' also appeared in *The turnrow Anthology of Contemporary Australian Poetry*, ed John Kinsella, turnrow press/ University of Louisiana at Monroe, 2013.

'What's Coming Next' also appeared in *Harbour City Poems*, ed Martin Langford, Puncher and Wattmann, Sydney, 2009.

'The Beautiful Anxiety' also appeared in *The Best Australian Poems 2008*, ed Peter Rose, Black Inc, 2008.

'The Future', 'Big Fun', 'A White Boat', 'In Air' also appeared in *Fires Rumoured about the City: Fourteen Australian Poets*, ed Kit Kelen, ASM (Association of Stories in Macao), 2009.

'This Is Not Dove Cottage' also appeared in *The Best Australian Poems 2010*, ed Robert Adamson, Black Inc, 2010.

'The Slide' also appeared in *The Best Australian Poems 2013*, ed Lisa Gorton, Black Inc, 2013.

'The Beautiful Anxiety' won the 2007 Booranga Poetry Prize.

Part of the sequence 'Six Temperamental Sonnets' was a commission by the Red Room Company for Arts Law Week, Sydney, 2008. My thanks to Johanna Featherstone.

Many thanks to David Musgrave and Ann Vickery for their help in seeing and making something final. And, as always, to Annette Willis for 'more than thought'.

www.ingramcontent.com/pod-product-compliance
Lightning Source LLC
Chambersburg PA
CBHW030852090426
42737CB00009B/1199